This is a book about a chair.

Actually, a clan of chairs,

with ancient ancestors, cousins, spitting images,

and loved ones who have passed on. . . .

Those chairs!

They appear in many places: sometimes alone,

sometimes together.

Sometimes people sit in them; other times

they just mark space and time.

The shape of the chair pushes up and out of the ground.

These sloped back legs have a dynamic thrust both in and out of the earth

that make us notice the chair. It digs into the ground. It leaves prints.

Early ones are big, clumsy, and hard to move.

They absorb water from the earth and the sky and they rot.

They appear on that road just outside Taos; those resorts in Guatemala,

Bali, and New Zealand; on that island off Vancouver; and in England—

and they are made by the thousands in China and Costa Rica.

What does the Adirondack chair really do?

Many things!

It holds us; sometimes it traps us.

One predictable part of my family gatherings in the mid-1950s

was the moment my Aunt Frances, a bit heavy and slightly arthritic,

would call for some help getting out of the Adirondack chair.

The chair brought my puny ten-year-old body in contact

with the aging, flabby arms of Great Aunt Frances:

a momentary, memorable embrace of the generations.

It flatters us.

It says: "My how good you look!

See how well we are all doing that we should have all this time to sit!

And such a nice place to sit.

Stay right there while I take your picture."

You probably have pictures like this, too.

It talks of summer

and our country

from sea to shining sea.

Adirondack chairs are like

painted wooden poems,

encapsulating and retrieving and

reshaping our memories.

It invites us to visit.

"Visiting" used to be a major activity.

Weekends were times to visit. There was some food and some talk and some of the very same talk (and maybe food) from the week before. Sometimes there was a predictable routine to the visits: how long, what to talk about.

In nice weather, you'd visit outside. These chairs were perfect.

We don't really visit that much any more by just sitting with someone.

There's usually a phone or a computer or an activity involved.

They are very easy to find.

Antique shops have sets, pairs, or loners.

Catalogs sell them for less than $200.

They begin "new" and start a life of use, get moved, worn, spilled on.

They get painted, get wiggly and then fixed, and rained on.

They hold snow in the winter and cats in the spring.

Squirrels perch on them to eat apples and stolen tulip bulbs.

They model for us that path from the new and the promising to the

regular, the invisible, the repaired, the old, and finally, the discarded.

★ 19

chapter 1

Introduction

T his is a book about a simple and humble chair form that shifts and slips around the country—and the world—on the winds of change. It is a chair rooted in the history of disease. It is a chair of the late industrial revolution, appearing only after new technologies began to distinguish time from life, the hobbyist from the tradesman. It is a chair related to efficiency and economy and waste. It is big and makes you feel comfortable and vulnerable. You must know that you are already safe before you can allow yourself to sit or stay seated in this chair. This is a chair intimately related to the assembly line and the consumer economy. Both early and contemporary versions can be made from packing crates or shipping pallets or recycled bottles. The Adirondack chair is a celebration of standardization, yet encourages individuation through its placement and use.

The simple Adirondack chair has become a domestic icon.

The chair is familiar—in the old sense of the term "family,"

  that collection of people, land, buildings, animals, and objects

 that constitute one's daily life.

   And as such, it isn't always popular—or let's say it goes in and out of favor.

For as long as I can remember, an Adirondack chair has been somewhere in somebody's yard. In 1952, a small one was just my size.

It is an object that has one basic form and many variations. The basic form is a deep, sloped seat with wide flat arms and back legs that angle up to meet the front legs. This is the shared DNA of the Adirondack chair clan. But the clinical dates or dimensions of the chairs are of lesser interest than the stories that surround them. The Adirondack chair has framed and propped the lives of four or five generations of Americans and has now made its way all over the world.

In the Catskill Mountains,

in the creek gorge behind a friend's house, it appeared.

An Adirondack-like chair had emerged from somewhere.

Clearly it was a rogue. It had gotten away from a porch, slipped beyond a backyard and

into the Kaaterskill Creek. Where it really came from, and where it went, I do not know.

All I know is I went looking for my daughter and her friend

and there they were in the spell of the chair.

"I must be the only person in America not obsessed with Adirondack chairs. Frankly, as an object, I'm more fascinated with the white molded plastic chair—you know the one that sells for $9. The Adirondack has isolationist arms with an awkward pitch which, depending on the version, is either not upright enough or not relaxed enough. As a Southerner, this 'just doesn't work' because of the typical Yankee stiffness. Since the

inception of the Adirondack, thousands of variations exist, some better than others, but I find they only look good in an empty field or at the edge of a lake—or better still, on a postcard . . . maybe the postcard is all we need!

Have you ever noticed how many retirement and financial planning advertisements have empty Adirondacks as a sign of enjoying the good life? . . . That life isn't for me. Are the chairs empty because everyone is dead or ran out of money? As I reflect on the Adirondack chair, it's a non-answer; it's like painting all the rooms in your house white."

—JOHN DANZER, FOUNDER OF MUNDER SKILES, NEW YORK

It's sometimes the perfect background.

It just sits and waits for something to happen to it. It holds space.

It seems to know how to cooperate with people, pets, sweaters, newspapers.

Recently the local feral cat beneath my barn has appropriated

one of my homemade Adirondacks.

Chairs, all chairs, are much more than just places to sit. They carry meanings that elude words. They very powerfully recall other times, places, and people. They have to do with remembering and forgetting, owning and disowning, living and dying. All of these things have brought me to the Adirondack chair. It has appeared like a spirit several times in my personal life and, more importantly, it has shadowed our national life throughout the twentieth century and now into the twenty-first, albeit in a sleek, extruded-plastic form.

The Adirondack chair is the quiet witness to our nation's recent history. This book is homage to that chair.

It has been about a hundred years since the appearance of an elegant recognizable form of what's now called the Adirondack chair. It was made just east of the Adirondack Mountains, in Westport, a town on the New York State shore of Lake Champlain. That original design, "the Westport Plank chair," was built from unusually wide, single boards and is now the least common variety found today. Mostly, people think of the Adirondack chair as a chair with "all the slats," but the earliest reference to that design is actually "the Cape Cod chair." Ambiguity is built into the very character of this chair—it's many things at once, both physically and metaphorically.

chapter 2

The Lineage of a Chair

The known history of chairs goes back to Egypt in 3000 BCE. Since then, most cultures have developed some form of the chair.

Indeed, the story of making the very first Adirondack chair begins in 1903 with the interest of Thomas Lee to make a suitable outdoor chair for his mother, described to me by her nephew as a "very large woman." Ah, the Matriarch's Throne!

Even in today's egalitarian society, the chair retains a quality of the throne, a center of power and privilege. Who among us cannot recall stories of "Dad's chair"? Remember Archie Bunker's chair? How many arguments start over chairs—which dining chairs we sit in, the best-

A chair is not a casual item, neither to make nor to live with.

It is all tied up with status, power, and honor.

positioned living room chairs, and the most comfortable porch chairs. Perhaps the most powerful of all fights are over who gets what chairs as a household is being broken up after death or divorce.

My daughter recently settled into her first apartment and announced that she only needed two chairs because there were only two people living in the apartment. She was unknowingly echoing Thoreau who called for at least three chairs: one for solitude, two for friendship, and three for society. Certainly there is an enormous difference in meaning between encountering one, two, and three chairs. One might be seen as lonely or isolated, two might seem exclu-

sive, and three does indeed seem to be the beginning of an invitation.

Design critic, and author of several design books, Ralph Caplan says that "a chair is the first thing you need when you don't need anything, and is therefore a peculiarly compelling symbol of civilization." The United States, in particular, has had a loony affair with chairs.

"*My parents were both Holocaust survivors. I was born in 1950, shortly after they came to this country. I grew up among ghosts—the memories and images of family I had never known. They made our house dark and foreboding. My parents had little, but they managed to arrange for us all to vacation in the Catskills every summer. There, among the scented pines and blue-painted swimming pools, it seemed that the ghosts could not find us. We could breathe here; we could even laugh. For my parents, the Catskills meant the promise of a future; proof that they had indeed escaped the world's worst nightmare. So they took great pains to document the time. Day after day my sister and I would pose together in the Adirondack chairs that we could both fit into. There's a whole roll of my father in the chair with my mother on the armrest. Then there's Mom in the chair and Dad leaning over to kiss her. There are photos of the chair upside down, with either my sister or I trapped underneath—a favorite game. There are even group photos of people I don't recognize, but that's okay. When I look at these pictures, my eye goes to the ever-present Adirondack chair and the peace and fun it promised. I have sat on these and stared at forests, I have spent hours in them gazing at the sea. I feel about these chairs as I do about the orange day lilies that grew so abundantly beside them. For me, they are about going home.*"*

—SANDY CHORON, AUTHOR AND EDITOR

An unusual rustic chair from the "rocker craze" of the 1870s.

Ever since the 1840s, when the industrial revolution permanently intoxicated the country, there has been a rush to invent and reinvent the perfect chair, the most versatile chair, always, the next chair. There is evidence of this even in the most rustic of chairs.

The chair above has a pair of helical coil springs that collapse a bit and wiggle around when sat upon. The springs are dated 1869 and mention the Shakers. They allow almost any simple side chair to become a delightful rocker. And the story goes on: the U.S. Patent Office is brimming with oddball chair designs.

★ THE FAMILY TREE ★

THE MORRIS CHAIR

The most prominent feature of the Adirondack chair is its sloped back and seat. It is clearly in the clan of "recliners" whose earliest relatives are the daybeds developed in the seventeenth and eighteen centuries. These wonders of engineering took on chairlike forms as mechanical reclining chairs with detachable, hidden, or recessed footrests. In 1813, the English architect William Fuller Pocock (1779–1849) designed the reclining patient

Sargent Mfg. Co.

814 & 816 Broadway, New-York.

These cuts are inserted merely to give you an idea, and to attract your attention. It takes a catalogue of 100 pages to illustrate and describe in detail, variety, and price what they represent.

Fig. 1.

Our great specialty is to supply everything that an Invalid needs; but a stock so large and varied as ours necessarily runs into comforts and luxuries that well folks want. Space for description is too limited here for anything more than a brief reference to the accompanying cuts, each of which represents a full variety of its respective class. Our Catalogue tells the whole story. **WE SEND IT FREE.** You run no risk in ordering goods from us. We are widely known. Everything Guaranteed. Money refunded, with cost of delivery, for anything claimed not equal to representation.

Fig. 2.

Fig. 1.—*Sargent's "Monarch" Reclining Chair.* It embraces every essential to make it perfect as an ordinary upright easy chair, or a reclining chair. It is adjustable to every position that either necessity or comfort requires, one of which is shown in Fig. 1, another in Fig. 11. We believe it to be the best in the world of its class, in every respect. Prices range, according to upholstery, from $80 to $125.

Fig. 2.—*Sargent's Regent Reclining Chair,* is a modification of the *Monarch,* varying somewhat in construction, but having practically its principal features. It is plain but equal in respect to quality and finish, and is withal a splendid chair for a moderate price. We make it both caned—to be used with or without cushions—and upholstered with springs and hair. Price, caned, $25; with loose cushions, $10 to $40 extra, according to quality. Price, upholstered, $35 to $60.

Figs. 3, 4, and 5 are representative cuts of our *Rolling Chairs,* of which we have all grades, sizes, and prices, from $16 up.

Fig. 4.   Fig. 5.

Fig. 3.

Fig. 6.

Fig. 6.—*Sargent's Solid Comfort Back Rest and Folding Bed Tray.* These are, indeed, of inestimable value in the sick-room. Prices, *Back Rests,* No. 1, plain, $4; No. 2, with arms, $5; No. 3, with head rests, $5; No. 4, with both arms and head rests, $6. *Trays,* No. 1, 15 x 25 inches, $3; No. 2, 17 x 28 inches, $4—in black-walnut or ash. Mahogany, $1 extra.

Fig. 7.—*Earth Closets.* Made under the Moule patents, which are unquestionably the best. Price, $35.

Fig. 8.—*Sargent's Sanitary Commode.* The only Commodes made which are absolutely odorless. We make all kinds as well. Prices, $5 to $25.

Fig. 7.   Fig. 8.   Fig. 9.

Fig. 9.—*The "Utility" Adjustable Folding Table.* Adjustable in height to suit any person or purpose. It is the only original "Utility" Table. Price, $6 up.

Fig. 10.—*Goodwin's Invalid Manipulator.* An attachment to any bed for the purpose of raising the whole body, or the back, or feet, or turning an invalid. It has afforded relief to many sufferers. Price, $50; with mattress, $58.

Fig. 11.—*Sargent's Table Universelle.* A marvel of utility and beauty for the library or sick-room.

Fig. 12.—*Sargent's Carrying Chairs.* The occupant can be comfortably carried up and down stairs. Prices, $10 to $25.

Fig. 13.—*Sargent's Invalid's and Fracture Bed.* Pronounced by the medical profession to be the most complete of anything ever invented for the purpose. Price, $125.

Fig. 10.   Fig. 11.

In addition to the above, we have Crutches, Physicians' Operating Chairs and Lounges, Exercising Chairs, Rubber Goods, Library Supplies, etc. Special appliances made to order. Correspondence invited. Send for our Catalogue. Address

SARGENT MFG. CO.

814 and 816 Broadway, N. Y.

The Robert Mitchell Furniture Co. are our agents in Cincinnati, O.

Fig. 12.

Fig. 13.

★ 39

Interesting Relation of Craftsman Oak and Willow Furniture

CRAFTSMAN HAND-MADE WILLOW FURNITURE is in no sense limited for use to the porch, the lawn or the bungalow. On the contrary, its design and finish is such as to make it equally appropriate in any room, whether bedroom, den or library. Especially is it constructed to serve in contrast with the darker and heavier oak furniture and offer the exact relief necessary to lighten the general effect. In fact, it lends itself so completely to The Craftsman way of furnishing that we have come to believe that a room requires one or two pieces to be entirely satisfactory.

The comfort of the user is as carefully considered in designing the willow furniture as it is in that of the usual Craftsman style. Although strongly and firmly made, each piece possesses the flexibility of a well woven basket and fits the body comfortably regardless of position. Being light in weight, the chairs and settles are easily moved— another decided advantage.

Craftsman willow furniture is the perfect showing of slender flexible withes woven into basket work, and the delightful human quality of a little irregularity, due to its being hand-made, adds greatly to its appearance. The style of finishing is also particularly attractive. The idea is, in the one color, a green, to give the effect of fresh young withes as they look when the sap first begins to flow in the spring, and in the other, the golden brown, to show the withes as they are seen later in the season.

The loose cushions can be covered with Craftsman canvas in tones of wood brown, dull, soft yellow or gray-green, and of course these coverings could be varied to suit any scheme of furnishing.

In brief the Craftsman Hand-Made Willow Furniture is on a par with all other Craftsman products for honesty of construction and beauty of design, and is practically indispensable to every lover of artistic home furnishing and decoration.

Send for our illustrated furniture catalogue, showing full line of willow pieces.

chair. Variations were developed throughout the nineteenth century, culminating in what is commonly called "the Morris chair," a reclining chair designed by William Watt and made in 1865 by Morris, Marshall, Faulkner & Co. The firm later became Morris and Company, the centerpiece of the English Arts and Crafts movement and the inspiration for both Gustav Stickley's Craftsman furniture and the work of his brothers, L. & J.G. Stickley. Both their various "arm chairs" and "reclining chairs" in the Morris style were very popular and copied by many American furniture companies at the time. Versions were mass-marketed in the Sears Roebuck and Montgomery Ward catalogs at the turn of the twentieth century. The Adirondack chair looks very much like a Morris chair dressed down for outdoor use.

Two versions of the popular Morris chair, with and without cushions.

★ 41

DECK CHAIRS

The Adirondack chair is an *outdoor* chair, and there are historical roots there, too. An outdoor version of the recliner was developed in the 1850s. It was the "deck chair" developed for use on the decks of ocean liners and other water-craft that carried passengers. What makes the early deck chairs interesting for this discussion is that they were meant to be outdoors.

Some were in an ✕ frame design with canvas seats. These are still used in some parks, such as these in London's Hyde Park.

PRIMITIVE CHAIRS

That angled leg appears in other kinds of furniture where there is the temptation to lean way back, bringing one dangerously close to tipping right back over. This beautiful primitive piece solves the problem just like the Adirondack chair does with those dynamic sloping legs. These are all interesting and important, but really minor influences compared to the influence of a particular kind of invalid furniture.

THE CURE CHAIR

It's unlikely that there would have been an Adirondack chair were it not for the tuberculosis epidemic—"The White Death"—that killed millions in the late nineteenth and early twentieth centuries.

Tuberculosis, once commonly known as "consumption" or "wasting," has been around for most of recorded human history. Traces of TB bacillus have been found in

Neolithic graves in Europe and even in Egyptian mummies. It is estimated that in the last two centuries alone, one billion people around the world have been killed by tuberculosis.

Early in the eighteenth century it was first theorized that TB might be contagious. A century later, it was discovered that fresh mountain air, rest, and lots of good food and milk seemed to be able to cure tuberculosis. (Although, in reality, less than 20 percent of those afflicted ever recovered.) Sanatoria and spas sprang up in many mountain regions, where tubercular patients could go for the "rest cure": usually three months of enforced rest, quarantined from the rest of the world, often sitting for hours wrapped in a blanket on a porch.

★ 45

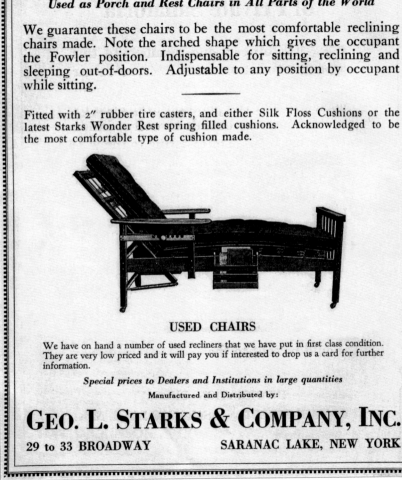

Sturdy, adjustable, and easily disinfected,

cure chairs became the standard sick bed for sanitoriums

in the United States and across Europe.

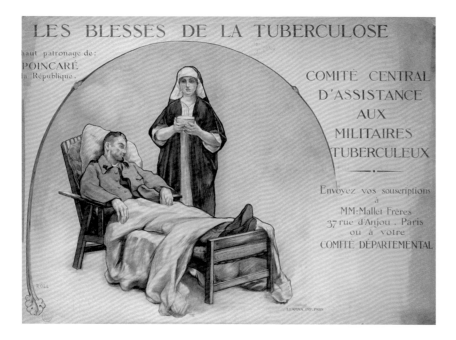

Special chairs were developed in the 1860s that made these long hours as comfortable and effective as possible. The chairs were often cushioned, adjustable, and had wide arms for books, writing pads, and dishes. These were known as "cure chairs" and they resembled a daybed.

The first successful tuberculosis sanatorium in the United States was started in 1884 in Saranac Lake, New York, a tiny wilderness village in the Adirondack Mountains. The town thrived on its new industry, drawing such famous patients as Robert Louis Stevenson, Walker Percy, Christy Mathewson, Norman Bethune, Rollo May, Stephen Crane, and Bela Bartok. Other, smaller "cure cottages" and board-ing houses were more affordable to people of more modest means.

Every residence had porches and chairs, and Saranac Lake earned the nickname "The Village of a Thousand Porches." This led several local furniture companies to produce their own versions of the cure chair called "The Adirondack Recliner" and the "'Rondack Combination Couch and Chair."

It is likely that these chairs inspired the simpler, cheaper plank and slat versions we know today. Indeed, in the original 1904 patent application for the Westport Plank chair, Harry C. Bunnell goes into great detail in both description and diagram about the appropriateness of this chair for "invalids." The

So the chair that was sat in for hours a day, by thousands of people,

became the icon of the region. Those wide arms,

that sloped back and seat: that was "the Adirondack chair."

patent drawing includes cushions and a compartment where a baseboard is stored, capable of making the chair into more of a lounger.

The sanatoria approach developed in Saranac Lake was duplicated in rural and mountain regions all over the United States and, like Saranac Lake, the entire economy of many other rural sanatoria towns across the country was built on treating tuberculosis.

By 1950, there were approximately 100,000 beds (and presumably chairs) available for tubercular patients, but by then, the disease had waned. There was better general public hygiene, a better understanding of contagion and, most importantly, the antibiotic streptomycin had been developed and found effective against TB. The choice of the "rest cure," with its high costs in money, distance, isolation, and boredom paled against a year or two's dosage of an anti-

biotic. Slowly, the sanatoria closed; their buildings reopened as general hospitals, prisons, and religious institutions. Some of the thousands of porch chairs lingered on, others wore out, were discarded,

or sold off. The two chairs Akiko Busch writes about in her book *The Uncommon Life of Common Objects* (page 58), were bought right off a porch in Saranac Lake by her grandmother.

chapter 3

The Chair from Westport, New York

In the early 1900s, Thomas Lee and his family, residents of Boston, had a large summer retreat in Westport, New York, on the shore of Lake Champlain. Like most big camps of the time, there were several buildings. One was Stony Sides, the other North Shore. Despite his summer residency, Lee was a major landowner and employer in the area. He owned the water company in the town, piping spring water—the then-famous Westport Spring Water—into the village and to a bottling plant. It is said that the water was so popular that Theodore Roosevelt had it served at the White House.

Family members recall that in the summer of 1903, Lee spent time tinkering with the design

The early Adirondack design has an unmistakable delicacy of line and form.

and prototypes for a comfortable lawn chair. All summer long, he kept adjusting angles and having family members (all 22 of them) try them out, one by one, until he got one that worked.

THE WESTPORT PLANK CHAIR

The results of Lee's tinkering were nothing more than unusual home-made family chairs until Lee and local carpenter Harry Bunnell (one local pronunciation seems to be

"Bru-nell") were hunting in the autumn of 1903. Bunnell mentioned how he was looking for some winter work and Lee suggested that Bunnell make some of those big chairs. Bunnell saw this as an opportunity. He modified Lee's original chair a bit and in April 1904 applied for a patent on what he called "a chair of the bungalow type adapted for use on porches, lawns, [and] at camps. [It is] a strong durable chair adapted to withstand rough usage and exposure to the weather."

The chairs were made from 20-inch-wide planks and measured 37 inches tall × 39 ⅝ inches wide × 38 ½ inches deep; the arms were 9 ½ inches wide. In July 1905, he received the patent.

"*My mother and father have been gone for years, but if I could meet them again, I would hope to find them at a cocktail party, in July, in the rose garden of our old house in upstate New York. It would be dusk and the flares would be lit, and we would sit in the white lawn chairs. The white lawn chairs. These are the words that say everything about those lost moments of a family. They are more evocative and more precise than any others. They are about languor and repose, and the exchanges that sometimes occur when one's mind is at rest. Like the cocktail party itself, they are about saying absolutely nothing and absolutely everything and about not knowing, perhaps until a later time, which is which. And they are about the great beauty of such confusions. What they describe, too, is the smooth assembly of planes. With their straight backs and long, wide arms gleaming white, the lawn chairs stand like small, immovable monuments, champions in the obscure garden of family relations.*

The chairs in our garden were salvaged by my grandmother from the porch of an old sanatorium in the Adirondacks. Multiple coats of white paint have long since covered the original brown or green. When I was growing up, my father pointed out to me repeatedly that if I leaned back in one of these chairs, rested my arms on its arms, and breathed deeply, I was positioned in such a way that I couldn't help but fill my lungs with air.

Every spring we would repaint them. When my sister and I were kids, we were given twenty-five cents each to do the job. Years later, when my boyfriend and I decided to get married, it happened to be in the spring, and there was nothing better I could think to do than give the chairs a new coat of paint.

At dusk, especially, their whiteness seems almost to glow like a sequence of bright flags. You could call them phantom furniture. And it is my great good fortune to have ghosts such as these in my garden. "
—AKIKO BUSCH, FROM *THE UNCOMMON LIFE OF COMMON OBJECTS*

★ 57

Harry Bunnell's home workshop in Westport, New York, where he made his chairs from 1905 to 1930.

Bunnell had a retail store on the main street in Westport and did the chair production in his basement shop in his house on Ledge Hill Road for the next few decades.

The original chairs were made of eleven pieces of hemlock or basswood and finished in either green or brown. The chairs were stackable. They originally sold for $4. At the time, Sears, Roebuck & Co. was offering simple dining chairs for as little as 45¢. An oak "Reclining Morris Chair" with upholstered cushions was $4.25. So the Westport Plank chair was a bit pricey in its day. By 1912 it was being featured in a furniture catalog in Saranac Lake, New York, for $10 (reprinted on page 60).

For twenty-five years, Harry Bunnell made and sold this chair and variations in the form of a children's chair, a loveseat for two, and a "Tete-a-Tete," throughout the Adirondack region. He stamped each of his chairs with his name, his town, and the patent date. In 1922, he got another patent for a "Convertible Chair." It featured the addition to the original chair of a pair of rockers that could be lowered and locked into place, creating a rocking chair version of his original Bungalow chair.

When Bunnell died in 1930, the production of chairs with his name stopped, but by then the chair form and its variations had begun to appear in other places.

It's still possible to find original Bunnell Westports around

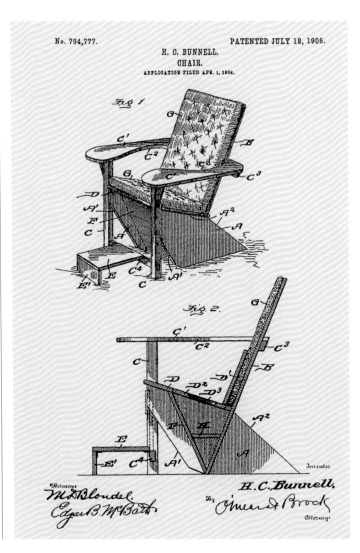

U. S. Patent, July, 18, 1905.
Canadian Patent, Feb. 5, 1907.

Adirondack Bungalow Chair
No. 3E121
$10

The simple, graceful lines, handsome exclusive design, rich appearance and luxurious, restful comfort, combined in this chair, appeal strongly to lovers of things that are oddly beautiful—besides being extremely comfortable.

The inventor certainly appreciated the advantages of tilting back a chair until the back and seat were at exactly the most comfortable angle; and he also evidently understood the disadvantage of exceeding that angle and falling over backwards; for in this chair he has obtained the limit of tilting comfort, with absolute safety.

Every inch of this chair is handmade from selected woods that grow in the forests of the Adirondack Mountains. It is constructed throughout, and handsomely finished in every detail, with extreme, painstaking care.

Try a couple of these chairs on your porch or in your library. Your family and your guests will prefer them to any other chair, outdoors or indoors, solely because they are so very, very restful. In these chairs you will also have something decidedly different and more desirable than those usually found elsewhere.

60 ★

today. They show up in antique shops, auctions, and even flea markets. The Adirondack Museum in Blue Mountain Lake, New York, offers a set of plans and there are several woodworkers specializing in these chairs. The most faithful is Ron Cosser of The Craftsman in Eastwood, New York, who works in mahogany. John Thayer has used an original Westport as his model. His chairs are made, not from basswood or hemlock, but more weather-resistant South American hardwoods with just a coat of teak oil.

chapter 4

From the Westport Plank to the Adirondack Chair

Bunnell built and sold his chairs for more than twenty-five years. They were beautiful, unique, and seemingly so simple. They very likely had an impact on the larger world of design.

WESTPORT STYLIZED

The most intriguing association is with a chair that appeared in Holland in 1918. It was an icon of a design movement known as de Stijl, which attracted a small but influential group of painters, poets, sculptors, and architects. The chair is, of course, designer Gerrit Rietveld's *Red and Blue Chair*. It is related to the Westport chair really only by the angle of the backboard to the seat. The chair itself is small and confining; it is delicate and

There are undeniable similarities between the Westport chair (1904) and this famous chair by Dutch designer Gerrit Rietveld (1918).

provocative in its lines and changing colors. The joinery was all on the surface. For Rietveld and de Stijl (which means "the style"), it was both a chair and an idea. That idea was the importance of using straight lines, right angles, obvious intersections, and color—red, blue, or yellow on a ground of white or black. These were the elements of harmony. The move-

ment, which lasted from 1917 to 1931, encouraged a multimedium expression of these guidelines in architecture, furniture, and painting, the most prominent painter being Piet Mondrian.

This would have been pretty heady stuff for Bunnell, a guy building plank chairs in his basement workshop. "Do you want green or brown?" he might ask. His Westport Plank chair was conceived for rough use, for the yard, for invalids. It was plain and sturdy. That was the idea. End of story.

It is possible that Rietveld had seen this Westport chair in the fourteen years it preceded his *Red and Blue Chair*. He was very familiar with the works of American architect Frank Lloyd Wright and had been asked to copy some of Wright's work for a client. Wright's own *Robie Chair* (1904) also featured a single plank angled back.

Frank Lloyd Wright's Robie Chair *of 1904.*

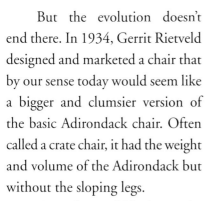

Rietveld's
1934 version.

But the evolution doesn't end there. In 1934, Gerrit Rietveld designed and marketed a chair that by our sense today would seem like a bigger and clumsier version of the basic Adirondack chair. Often called a crate chair, it had the weight and volume of the Adirondack but without the sloping legs.

Even if Rietveld had seen the Westport chair, he exercised the most fundamental artistic process. He changed it in such a way that it took on new or different or greater meaning. He filleted that big Ameri-can bruiser of a chair and brought it down to a lovely colored skeleton.

Sometimes "inspiration" is not so dramatic. In 1927, Italian architect Gino Levi Montalcini from Turin produced a teak lounge chair that was very close in design to the Westport chair. He thinned the arms down and made the seat and the back each from two rather than one piece of wood. Westport chair inventor Thomas Lee spent quite a bit of time in Italy in 1923, which may explain how that chair form appeared there.

Even a battered and worn chair is inviting.

ADIRONDACK CHAIRS

BY JOY KATZ

At dusk they've scraped themselves off the brick—they rise, yes—
they are ready—a readiness, a preparedness: they are certainly
not chairs. Boats' composure: how boats look,
complete without you. Boats want for wind but not sailors,
look like they wait for wind, becalmed. Empty chairs don't need us.

★ 67

"People often place Adirondack chairs near each other, but they aren't social furniture. Even in catalogs, Adirondack chairs are empty. At an artists' colony in New Hampshire, I encountered a few Adirondack chairs at the edge of a field. No one ever sat in them. Just after sunset they glowed white, like a kind of huge bird getting ready to take off. The chairs in this poem were in my garden in California."

—JOY KATZ, AUTHOR OF *FABULAE* AND *THE GARDEN ROOM*

sented in hickory saplings with the bark still on. The seat was a woven rattan. Visually, it was a very successful interpretation of the Westport and retained all the comfort of the original.

In 1960, Lester Collins, the famous American landscape architect, took the spirit of Rietveld's chair and interpreted it for a grand garden, Innisfree, which he was building in Millbrook, New York. (It is now open to the public from May through October.) Collins's chair is now the popular "Wave Hill chair" available for sitting and buying at the Wave Hill Arboretum on the Hudson River, in Riverdale, New York.

WESTPORTS CLONED

Most simply, the Westport Plank chair or the Bungalow chair was just plain copied.

In 1913, Ransom Eli Olds, the prolific automobile inventor of the

A RUSTIC COUSIN

In the 1930s, a major producer of rustic furniture, The Old Hickory Furniture Company of Shelbyville, Indiana, introduced a rustic version of the Westport chair. Instead of planks and milled wood, the features of the Westport were pre-

REO and the Oldsmobile, founded a new city in Florida, which he named R. E. Olds-on-the-Bay. (The town is now called Oldsmar. It was a dreamer's plan with the city laid out in a grid to resemble Washington, D.C., and the streets paved with oyster shells. As part of his plan there was a sawmill that, in addition to lumber, produced what was called "the Olds chair," made from wide boards of cypress or yellow pine. It is claimed that they were sold and shipped, but only one has reappeared. This is a child's-size chair in the collection of the City of Oldsmar. In 1923, Olds sold off his stake in the city after losing more than three million dollars.

WESTPORTS REPAIRED

Often designs move by accident. No matter how durable a chair is, it can break or succumb to weather. Chair repair is an ongoing activity.

It is likely that, in addition to being copied and used for inspiration, the Westports were just simply fixed as they aged. That big single plank was replaced with several slats from a packing crate or another few boards. If the back started to wiggle, some engineering-minded hobbyist thought of adding a few extra braces in the back.

The Coming of the Adirondack Chair

The history of furniture, and particularly furniture in the United States, is to keep improving: *more*

comfort, more versatility and durability, less weight, different materials.

It's an intriguingly simple process. "What can I do to make this better?"

The original Westport or Bungalow chair was a masterpiece of design. But one man's design is just another's challenge. So if the look of the chair was not drop-dead important, then there was tremendous opportunity to tinker. And that's just what happened.

Making an authentic Westport, required at least four 20-inch-wide boards. This was not impossible, but if one was not wed to that particular feature, then just any set of boards could work. The Montalcini teak version of 1927 had two 9- or 10-inch boards and the Collins chair of 1960 used the same.

But if two, why not three or four? And so it happened. That slightly pricey, fussy Westport Plank

chair was democratized. It was reduced to a set of plans that absolutely any modest woodworker could execute—and stamp with his own personal design mark—with simply found or cheaply bought lumber.

chapter 5

The Right Chair at the Right Time

The Adirondack chair is both a chair-to-buy and a chair-to-make, which has helped make it so unusually popular. That is not the case with any other chair I can think of. There were several trends bubbling in the United States at the turn of the twentieth century that seemed to favor the Adirondack chair as an item to own and consume as well as an item to make for yourself.

The American Frontier had closed in the 1890s and the new frontier was not as much "moving on" as it was acquiring a degree of personal independence: a house of one's own, a comfortable living, and the time, thanks to labor-saving devices and certain labor laws, to relax and simply enjoy life.

The Adirondack chair became a safe outpost in the yard or on the beach.

Most visibly, between 1890 and 1930, the number of privately owned homes tripled—there were more houses, porches, and yards than ever. Via the automobile, people were leaving the crowded row houses and apartments of the cities to live in the newly emerging suburbs. With increased private home ownership, home decoration became more important. Alan Gowans, in *The Comfortable*

House, mentions three themes that were reflected in the actual styles of the houses and house plans being offered. He says that people responded to issues of security: a house should be a defense, a safe retreat from the world. Second, within the house there should be some connection with the richness of the American past, particularly the Colonial period. Third, the house should help reestablish a

The Adirondack chair is a small icon of home.

sense of family stability, which had been fractured by the demands of the contemporary workplace.

Each of these characteristics is worth looking at a bit more closely, even in a discussion of the Adirondack chair. The home-as-haven concept was an important part of a social reform movement, which was concerned about the debilitating effects of industrialization after the breakup of the agrarian base of America. One concern, of many, was the effect of the shift of work away from the home or homestead to a factory or office. One way to restore the importance of the home was to emphasize it as a haven, a personal retreat from the demands of the work world. So "home" was the place, the safe place, where you could be more yourself, resting, playing, working at your own pace and time, possibly with other members of the family. This essentially turned the home into a kind of small "factory" where you still "worked"—but just on different projects. This was actually the beginnings of the Do-It-Yourself movement, which justified and often mandated that the man of the house be handy, that he be working on projects around the house.

Since the early 1980s, the Adirondack chair has made a big comeback.

They more or less disappeared in the 1960s and 1970s

when more modernist outdoor furniture was popular.

TRIPLE THREAT

BY DONALD LEVIN, FROM *IN PRAISE OF OLD PHOTOGRAPHS*

Reproducing old photographs
of my young father—his twenties
and thirties an unknown country
and him still healthy, slender and
sepia, hair slicked back, casual in
an Adirondack chair, legs crossed,
cigarette smartly posed,
or standing in white duck trousers
with a crease as sharp as his prospects,
athlete's body still strong and lithe
before the ailments of adulthood
clobbered him, those of the body
and, after, those that followed in
the shame that sequeled its wake
and left him gasping and grateful
for any woman's attention,
my mother's in particular,
and made him surrender all
the sharp and dark young man had been
to her, to children and work and
crushing, endless debt so he could gain

something close to the normal life
that he never felt he deserved—
for Father's Day I selected
three photos from the high school sports
he excelled in, baseball, football,
especially track, and made a
triptych of these, Triple Threat,
I called it, which he bent over,
holding his most powerful
magnifying glass close to his
practically sightless eyes in
century-old stiff and useless hands,
this reminder of the vigor
that had once been his to squander,
and asked why I hadn't also
duplicated the newspaper
articles, the ones that called him
the schoolboy sensation, record
wrecker, "Flash Levine," as they misspelled
it, one of the greatest sprinters
ever to step on a board track.

Did I have that one? And would
I make a copy of it, and send
it right back to him? Right away?
I said I would, and he cast
his dim eye over the display
happy for something to show
his friends what his early life was like,
convinced no one would believe him
without such evidence, like
a condemned man who finds at last
some proof he once was free.

"*When I think of Adirondack chairs I immediately think of the photograph of my father, Nathan Levin, as a young man in his thirties, seated in an Adirondack chair in front of the enormous grill of an old sedan, gazing out with a rakish grin as though relaxing before joining a party at Gatsby's. The chair, and this photo, are at the heart of the poem* Triple Threat. *I have always associated the clean and sturdy lines of Adirondack chairs with both the sense of possibilities represented for me by this picture, and the athleticism of my father's early years that the poem remembers.*"

—DONALD LEVIN, AUTHOR

Now! . . . Fresh Air . . . and Relaxation

$4⁵⁹

3-Piece Set

No need to postpone summer comfort! The price of this lawn set is so low, you can buy gay accessories with the money you save. True Adirondack style—husky enough for years of good, sturdy service. Deep and comfortable with fan backs and seats slanted at the correct angle. Made of hardy, smooth Douglas Fir, well sanded, ready to paint. Use Sears colorful enamels or varnish for fine results. Extra wide arms. 7¼ in. wide. Handy for refreshments, books etc. Chair seat. 18¾x16½ in. Settee seat. 38½x16½ in. Ht. of backs, 31½ in. Hexagonal table top. 25½ in. 3 sturdy legs. 27½ in. high. Easily set up. Nails not included. Mailable. Save more by ordering the 3-piece set!

1 L 1103—**Chair.** Shipping weight. 22 pounds....................$1.29
1 L 1104—**Settee.** Shipping weight. 38 pounds...................2.19
1 L 1108—**Table.** Shipping weight. 19 pounds................... 1.29
1 L 1109—**3-Pc. Set:** Settee and Two Chairs or Settee, Table and Chair as shown. **State choice.** Shpg. wt., 82 lbs.......................$4.59

This was an absolutely new idea in American culture. Men, of all classes, after the demise of the farm-homestead, were not caretakers of the house. There were professionals hired to do the repairs. With this increase in private home ownership, and several other characteristics, the stage was set for men to start grazing for projects.

"Traditional values" were very important at the turn of the last century. Not only was there an architectural and decorative revival of the Colonial style, but more subtly, the yeoman values of self-reliance and self-sufficiency were being stressed. The American Arts and Crafts movement by 1915 was trivial as a political influence, but was still quite potent as an inspiration for the integrity of honest hard work, evoking the guilds of medieval Europe at a time when the factories were fracturing work into repeated, monotonous tasks.

Keeps Him Out of Trouble

I HAVE been a regular subscriber to your magazine for over a year and read it from cover to cover. It is the best magazine of its type ever published. I always make some project described in each issue and now it looks like we would need a larger house to hold everything. If more men would only take up a hobby of this kind they would get more fun out of life and have less time left to worry or get into trouble!

Dr. L.M.H., Suffield, Conn.

So, at a time when most of the workforce was in the employ of companies, there was a call for the romantic return to the rugged characteristics of the pioneers. As historian Steven M. Gelber says: "If a man could take care of his own home and build his own furniture, he had special resources with which to face the vicissitudes of life." There was a new stress on the corruptibility of the physical environment and the key role of the homeowner in staving off breakdown and decay.

A letter to the editor in Woodcraft Magazine, *September 1931.*

So this Adirondack chair, called the Cape Cod chair in the early hobby plans of the 1930s, offered the homeowner a rather fast, easy response to the growing pressure to perform as a newly competent handy man. It only took an afternoon or two and required only a hammer and a hand saw. To assist the hobbyist, there were national woodcraft clubs with local chapters. This kind of productive, social, busy work was seen as the mark of a well-balanced life.

THE HOME SHOP PROJECT

The Adirondack chair remains one of the most popular home shop projects, with plans readily available from catalogs, magazines, and the internet. For people needing more hands-on help, there are regular how-to demonstrations at local home-improvement centers and chair-building classes at local craft centers and community colleges: the chairs always seem to get themselves made!

SIDE BUSINESS

Right from the start, beginning with the spirit of Harry Bunnell and his Westport chair, the Adirondack chair has appealed to the entrepreneur. Historian Steven Gelber talks about this as the "job you can't lose." That tradition is still quite vital today: a farmer near me makes these chairs, one at a time, as part of his "winter work"; a carpenter on Block Island, Rhode Island, has been making "the Block Island Sittin' chair" for years.

Antiques dealer John Wicks of Johnson, New York, can remember that when he was a boy in the early 1930s these chairs, then called "the Catskill chair," would be brought through town for sale off the back of an old truck. This is not unlike the way I bought some similar chairs off the back of a truck in the late 1980s from Indians from Pennsylvania.

What's so interesting about this chair is its many identities. It seems to take on the names of the places it's found. A Westport chair seen in Delaware became "the Comstock chair" of Rome, New York. That story repeats itself.

84 ★

No matter what route you take to the Adirondack Mountains,
you'll find some roadside shop selling chairs.

THE LA-Z-BOY CONNECTION

In 1928, two cousins with a small furniture business just north of Monroe, Michigan, added a couple hinges to a wood-slat lawn chair and built the first automatic recliner. A year later Edward Knabusch and Edwin Shoemaker padded and upholstered their invention, and

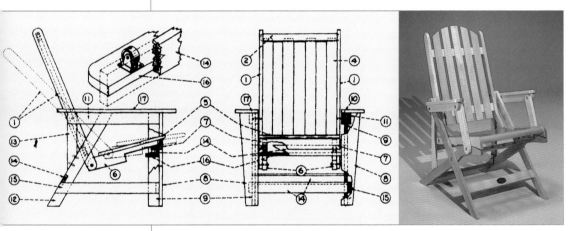

marketed it as the LA-Z-BOY. Today it is one of the best-selling chairs in American history. Notice the striking resemblance between Adirondack chair plans published in the 1920s and the original LA-Z-BOY model.

The Muskoka Chair

It was in the early 1930s when a round-backed version of the Adirondack chair appeared in the Muskokas, a resort area on the lakes in northern Ontario. The chair was a departure from the rather boxy Cape Cod style that was popular in the how-to magazines.

It has a rounded, contoured back and gathered waist to make it look more dynamic. Often the individual slats were painted in different or contrasting colors. This chair style is still very popular in Canada and very quickly made its way back across the border and was a featured style in the Sears Roebuck and Montgomery Ward catalogs of the 1930s and '40s. The chairs sold for $2.39 each. Today that style is called "the Kennebunkport chair," named after the resort town in Maine.

Small- and Large-Scale Production

The Adirondack chair is very well-suited to production work, whether in the home shop or the factory. Once a design is set on, the only chores are making all the components and assembling them.

The Amish in the Midwest produce these chairs by the truckloads for garden centers across the

ROARING LION CHAIR COMPANY, VERNON TOWNSHIP SCHOOL DISTRICT

In 1991, Jim Quinlan, an energetic, imaginative industrial arts teacher in rural New Jersey had an idea. For a variety of reasons, his woodworking class was being filled with students who were learning disabled, physically disabled, or labeled as having behavioral problems. For many it was just an available time slot on their schedules.

Quinlan decided to do something that would equip them with some of the skills necessary to survive in the workplace. "As most of us know, workplace survival is not simply a matter of performing a task," says Quinlan. "It involves interacting socially, working independently, accepting responsibility, and problem solving as well."

Quinlan chose the Adirondack chair as the way to help make this happen. He created the Roaring Lion Chair Company, and each year a new class of students produced and sold 50 Adirondack chairs. The students learned a variety of practical skills in the process.

Each student was paired with tasks appropriate to his or her abilities, and the company always turned a profit in money, goodwill, and a growing self-esteem among a fragile student population.

Chairs were sold locally, and in 1991, one was sent to President George H.W. Bush, who has it at his home in Kennebunkport, Maine.

"Unfortunately, many developmentally disabled individuals spend much of their adult lives isolated from the community," says Quinlan.

"This project is a remarkable testimony to the powers hidden within a simple object: the Adirondack chair, when seen in a new way."

Student Operated
at
Vernon Township High School   875-7111

The Roaring Lion

Chair Company

. . . MAKERS OF QUALITY ADIRONDACK CHAIRS
since 1991

country, and there are several furniture factories that produce them for the major retail and catalog sellers.

There are more and more Adirondack chairs imported from all over the world. There's a Costa Rican factory making teak Adirondack chairs. China sent 45,000 chairs to the United States a few years ago as a give-away premium for a tobacco company.

BACK TO THE HOME MADES

This outsourcing and off-shore production has kept the price of the chairs quite low. If you were to go to a lumberyard today and get the materials to make a generous version of the chair, the materials alone would cost about $70. So like many do-it-yourself projects,

An Adirondack chair from marante wood, made in China and "free" after buying 290 packages of cigarettes.

★ 91

the money-saving aspect is not always important. You can usually buy a chair cheaper than you can make one. Clearly there's something more to this chair form that appeals to the builder in all of us.

Fit only for the Fire: The Adirondack Chair

By Michael Kernan

They are actually bringing back the Adirondack chair. Not only is it showing up at your more elegant outdoor furniture stores alongside the yacht chairs and swimming pool loungers, but I now see it in some of our mail order catalogs. The chairs are billed—you knew they would be—as "classics" that bring back the great days of the turn-of-the-century Adirondack resorts. They are made of oak and "can be painted." Many folks love them, but personally I cannot imagine what would possess even the most yuppie-crazed merchandiser to bring back the Adirondack chair. They weigh about a ton, so you can't take them up on the porch to paint them in the spring, which means you paint them where they stand on the lawn, lifting up their feet to put newspapers underneath. Which means that for the rest of the summer they have little shoes of torn newspaper painted white or green, except where spears of grass got in the way.

Lifting up their "feet" I said. That's another thing—their so-called feet are one-by-six foot boards with raw edges that sink into your lawn like giant chisels. I know because I was the one who had to rearrange the chairs for my mother's lawn parties. If you wanted to pull your chair up close to someone, you had to stand, turn around, grab it with both hands and yank, ripping up telltale parallel divots in the turf.

When you sat in them you slid straight back until the front of the seat (another raw-edged board) hit you just below the knees. Your spine was forced straight up and out by the most unforgiving chair back this side of Louis XVI. Furthermore, the chair's generously broad arms were slanted down to the headrest. The instant you put a wet iced-tea glass down, it would slide towards you aiming to dump ice cubes in your lap.

I inherited two family Adirondack chairs when I got married and used them for kindling that same winter. They burned pretty good.

chapter 6

So You Want to Build an Adirondack Chair?

T here are many ways to do so. The best way to build one depends on how you best learn. Some like the seeming clarity of kits with precut pieces or plans and the security of step-by-step instructions. Some like watching a video or actually working in a class with a teacher and other students at a community college or woodworking or craft school. And then some of us like figuring it out on our own by just making it up or perhaps having a chair nearby to copy.

For people who like plans, John Wagner's helpful book, *Building Adirondack Furniture*, offers a good, clear set of step-by-step directions that result in a strong, generous sized chair and one that is easily personalized. He has kindly shared these drawings to help you get started. There are more details in his book.

A sturdy Adirondack chair is an eight- to ten-hour shop project.

ASSEMBLING THE BACK

Step 1. The Bottom Brace: Lay the five back slats next to each other. Lay the bottom back brace on top of them at one end. Position one back slat at each end of the brace. Square the edges. For both slats, predrill for two screws, making sure to align the holes on a diagonal to avoid splitting the wood. To make the screw holes symmetrically diagonal, drive them 1 inch in from each edge. (You'll use this method for all five slats.)

Once you have the holes drilled, insert two #8 1½-inch wood screws in both slats. Now, evenly space the three center slats between the two slats you've just installed. Given the width of your boards, the distance between the five slats will be about ⅝ inches. Once evenly spaced, predrill two diagonally placed holes at the end of all three slats and drive in the screws.

Step 2. The Top Brace: Place the top back brace 8 inches down from the top of the back slats. Use a square to position it. Predrill two holes at the end of both outside slats and screw into place. (When predrilling, make the same diagonal pattern that you made along the bottom brace.)

Recheck the ⅝-inch spacing. Predrill and screw the remaining three slats into place, maintaining the same diagonal screw pattern you established earlier.

Several simple strips of wood and a couple tools
are all that is needed to make your own chair.

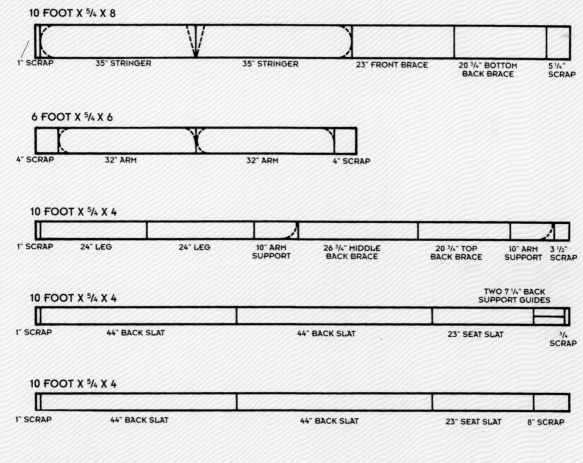

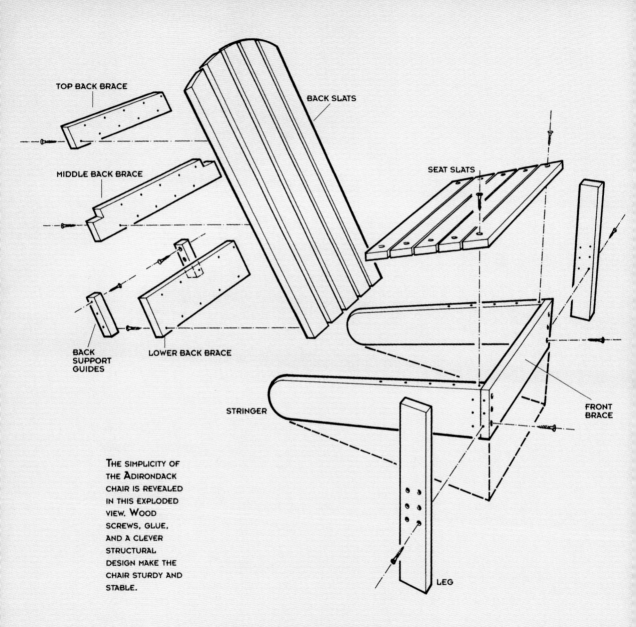

TOP BACK BRACE

BACK SLATS

MIDDLE BACK BRACE

SEAT SLATS

BACK
SUPPORT
GUIDES

LOWER BACK BRACE

STRINGER

FRONT
BRACE

LEG

THE SIMPLICITY OF
THE ADIRONDACK
CHAIR IS REVEALED
IN THIS EXPLODED
VIEW. WOOD
SCREWS, GLUE,
AND A CLEVER
STRUCTURAL
DESIGN MAKE THE
CHAIR STURDY AND
STABLE.

Step 3. The Middle Brace:
The placement of the middle back brace is crucial because its height determines the height of the chair arms. Since the arms will be parallel to the ground, place the bottom edge of the middle brace 18⅝ inches up from the bottom of the slats.

Center the middle back brace across the five back slats so that approximately 3 inches of the middle brace protrude from both sides. Make sure the middle brace is square to the slats, the bottom brace, and the top brace. Predrill and screw the brace into place. Stagger the screws diagonally as done on the other two braces.

Put the chair back aside.

ASSEMBLING THE STRINGER
Step 1. Installing the Front Brace:
We've already cut the front end of each stringer with a 75-degree angle and cut half circles at the back ends.

Predrill three holes ½ inch in from each end of the front brace: one in the center (about 3⅝ inches in from either edge), and the other 1⅝ inches in from the top and bottom edges. Hold the front brace up to the angled ends of the stringers and drive in the screws. Be sure the top of the brace is flush with the tops of the stringers.

Step 2. Installing the Front Legs: Turn the assembly on its side and insert a temporary spacer between the two stringers to support the structure.

Take one of the front legs and make a mark at 15 inches. Lay the leg so that its front is flush with the front of the front brace. Align the top of the front brace with the 15-inch mark on the leg.

Predrill and screw in six screws: three through the leg and the end grain of the front brace, and three through the leg and the side of the stringers. As always, stagger these screws slightly to avoid splitting.

Repeat this procedure to attach the second front leg.

INSTALLING THE BACK

Step 1. Marking the Back Placement: Before installing the chair's back, you'll need to make a few measurements. The depth of the chair seat should be 18 inches. Measure 18 inches back from the front brace and mark both stringers. Next, place a protractor on the inside of the stringer, and draw a line along the 100-degree edge. (The chair's back will tilt at a 100-degree angle.)

Step 2. Attaching the Back: Insert the assembled back between the stringers. Align the assembled back along the 100-degree guidelines and position its bottom to be even with the underside edge of the stringer. With an assistant holding the back in place, drill and screw three screws in each side. Screw from the outside of the stringer into the bottom back brace (not the slats).

Position the two precut 2 × ¾ back-support guides snuggly behind the bottom back brace into the two corners. Working from the inside, predrill and screw these blocks into the stringer. Use three screws in each block.

INSTALLING THE ARMS

The two protruding ends of the middle back brace will act as support for the chair arms, but you'll need to flatten this surface so that the arms can sit level.

Measure a ¾ inch down from the highest point of the middle back brace and make a mark on the end grain. Use a level to draw a level line through this mark. Then, mark off a ¾-inch space between the chair arm and the back slats.

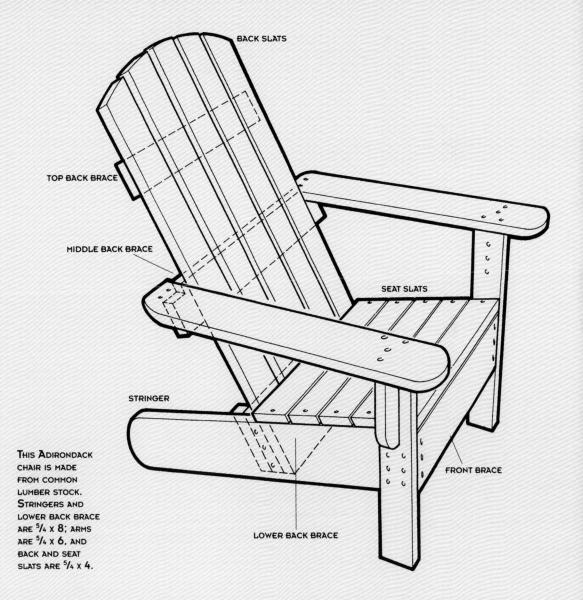

BACK SLATS

TOP BACK BRACE

MIDDLE BACK BRACE

SEAT SLATS

STRINGER

FRONT BRACE

LOWER BACK BRACE

This Adirondack chair is made from common lumber stock. Stringers and lower back brace are $^5/_4$ x 8; arms are $^5/_4$ x 6, and back and seat slats are $^5/_4$ x 4.

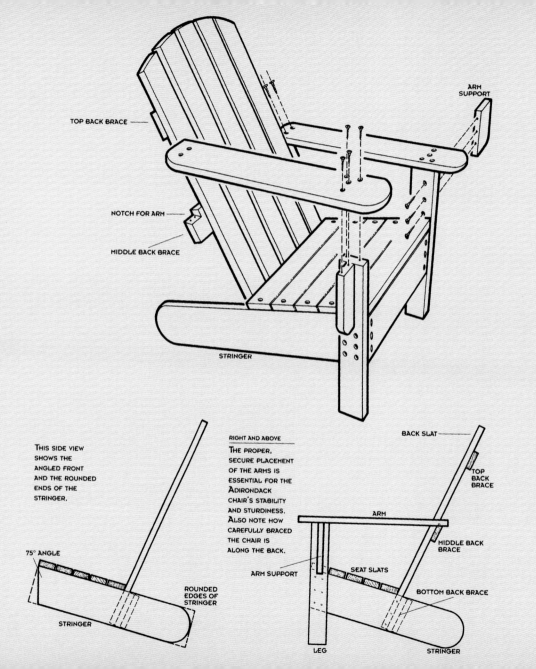

ARM
SUPPORT

TOP BACK BRACE

NOTCH FOR ARM

MIDDLE BACK BRACE

STRINGER

THIS SIDE VIEW
SHOWS THE
ANGLED FRONT
AND THE ROUNDED
ENDS OF THE
STRINGER.

RIGHT AND ABOVE
THE PROPER,
SECURE PLACEMENT
OF THE ARMS IS
ESSENTIAL FOR THE
ADIRONDACK
CHAIR'S STABILITY
AND STURDINESS.
ALSO NOTE HOW
CAREFULLY BRACED
THE CHAIR IS
ALONG THE BACK.

BACK SLAT

TOP
BACK
BRACE

ARM

MIDDLE BACK
BRACE

75° ANGLE

ROUNDED
EDGES OF
STRINGER

ARM SUPPORT

SEAT SLATS

BOTTOM BACK BRACE

STRINGER

LEG

STRINGER

With a handsaw, make careful cuts. Then, use a 1-inch chisel to chip away excess wood until the notch is accurate and smooth.

Lay the arm in place. Drill and screw two screws down into the front leg. Then drill and screw two screws into the notch. Angle your screws when screwing the back end of the arm in place.

Repeat on the other side.

Installing the Arm Supports

Center and square an arm support under an arm on the outside of a front leg. From the side, drill and screw three screws through the front leg and into the arm support. Position the screws so that they are centered and equidistant from both each other and the ends of the arm support.

From above, predrill and screw two more screws through the arm and into the arm support.

Repeat on the other side.

Installing the Seat Slats

Lay out all five seat slats, evenly spacing them on the stringers. Leave about ⅛ inch between each slat. Predrill and screw them into place. Use only one screw for each end of each slat.

| # Contemporary Makers

There are weekend woodworkers and hobbyists, and then, of course, there are the obsessed. They like tools; they like building. They like modifying designs. The motto is "Always Improve." These men and women are the relentless force behind dizzying numbers of adaptations, interpretations, and doodling with the humble Adirondack chair.

Perhaps it is *because* of its simplicity that the Adirondack chair has intrigued skilled craftsmen. There seems to be an endless number of variations in materials, design features, methods of assembly, and finishing. So many things can be done to the style. It can be redesigned over and over again, and yet it still remains so recognizable!

Artists and furniture makers all over the world have been inspired by the Adirondack's form.

WOODWORKERS EYE
THE LOWLY ADIRONDACK CHAIR

Andrew Jackson has developed more than fifty variations of the Adirondack chair in the last ten years, making him likely the most prolific Adirondack chair designer in the world! He varies both materials and design, and of his work, he says:

> I design Adirondack chairs. I am searching for new shapes, new possibilities, for things that have never been seen. But not just for newness, but for awesomeness: shapes and possibilities so resonant with some inner longing, and so visually striking that one would say that they are 'saturated with being.'
>
> I take an existing design, study it until I know (or think I know) how to improve it, and then build something new. Then I

repeat this process several more times. Since I cannot possibly actually build all of the chairs this process requires, I rely on manipulating photographs and building models of the developing designs. I do not rely on the opinions of others in this process, but only what my heart tells me. This is necessarily an entirely solitary and lonely process.

Tyler Donald of Pennsylvania

has developed two elegant forms of the chair.

He remembers such chairs at his great grandmother's house

on Upper Saranac Lake, New York.

Many other traditional makers

share Jackson's drive to change the design.

" I see this driftwood easy chair as a beachcomber's bit of stylish, homemade comfort. There's an allure and mystique surrounding the image of the beachcomber, that resonates with most of us. The rugged individualist who chucks the Puritan work ethic for a life of beauty, simplicity, barefoot freedom, and outdoor adventure. Huck Finn meets Jimmy Buffet. Jeremiah Johnson with a surfboard.

There are beachcombers all over the world, from the Caribbean to the South Sea islands. But this chair was inspired by my all-too-brief taste of the life when I lived among the ingenious and hardy beachcombers of Shi Shi beach on the extreme northwest tip of the Olympic Peninsula. They lived there year-round, and when they weren't feasting from their ocean pantry they were often creating: rough-hewn beach sculptures, functionally-beautiful rustic cabins, furniture and implements, fantastic swirling hearths made of beach stones, even intricate board games rich with beach life narrative ("Percy the Packrat craps in your granola. Lose three food points and two sanity points.").

These unchained souls were forced to don shoes and move to town or find another lonesome beach when this isolated shore was incorporated into the Olympic National Park in the late '80s. The ramshackle villas were torn down and wilderness was restored. Ah, between the well-planned extremes of commercial development and wilderness restoration, the unintentional paradise that the carefree beachcomber can claim as home is fading away into cultural mythology along with dinosaurs, the Old West, and our wonder years. "

—KAM GHAFFARI, FURNITURE DESIGNER

★ III

II2 ★

The Adirondack chair style is a popular exercise
in many design and architecture schools and woodworking programs.
In 2005, Indiana University of Pennsylvania held an exhibit
of student-designed and constructed chairs
inspired by the Adirondack form.

" *Life in coastal Maine is much more oriented to the outdoors and, of course, the water. Little by little, you find your interests and activities becoming more affected by the change of the seasons and the light. The architecture, the fishing piers, all these things began to creep into my consciousness and I became interested in designing a line of outdoor furniture. I like contrast in all kinds of things—I think it adds an element of drama to life, like spicy food. I like the rounded, volumetric form for a chair seat, and it seemed natural to me to pair it with a chair back that was flat. When I was working out how to attach the back to the seat I realized that I could make it adjustable just by creating a cantilever, and without using any hardware. What excited me most, and still does, is that the function of the chair merged with the form in a very simple way.* "

—Julie Morringello, furniture maker, Maine

THE ADIRONDACK IN ART

Artists have always rummaged through the stuff of popular culture. They see and understand, and they appropriate the commonplace. What they say about the power of an object makes it all the more visible.

Chairs have always held a special place in painting. Portraits are often done with people in chairs that are specially selected. The chair is one more reflection of the person who sits in it. Even an empty chair has held great interest for artists: Picasso, Monet, Tissot, Gauguin, Bonnard, and many others have used one as a central feature in their paintings.

It should be no surprise that artists have appropriated the Adirondack chair form with gusto in recent years. The Adirondack chair is most often seen in landscape paintings (and photographs) as a marker of a journey, of rest, or of longing. Sometimes there are more ominous meanings tucked in, perhaps abandonment and decay. And then there's a whole vein of Adirondack chair art that is simply intrigued with the lines and angles of the chair. Colorado sculptor Paul Jacobsen creates colorful gaggles of small Adirondack chairs as dynamic wall pieces.

There are many unconventional makers, like myself.

If you think of the back of an Adirondack chair

as needing just anything flat to lean against,

it takes you to odd places,

like Jimmy Howard's Sled Back Adirondack,

or one I made out of an array of worn canoe paddles,

or ones made from reclaimed pallets or skis or slabwood.

Sometimes the chair itself

can be transformed

into a work of art.

THE GREEN CHAIR

One of the more interesting appearances of the Adirondack chair was in a form called the Green Chair. As the story goes, it was 1991 in a poor, drug-ridden section of Minneapolis,

Minnesota. A chair, an Adirondack chair, was stolen off the porch of a home. Neighbors and artists Joel Sisson and Chris Hand thought what better way to address the notion of a coveted item than to make more

and more of these chairs and give them away. So began the Green Chair Project, named after the paint color used on the finished product. Sisson and Hand got together a group of local youngsters to build 90 chairs to give to everyone in the neighborhood. In the process, everyone learned about building, business, and community. The project continued for several years, offering plans and advice on how to establish a similar program in other places. In 1995, four giant 12-foot Green Chairs were installed as sculpture in four parks in the Twin Cities area,

each weighing 2,500 pounds and standing as reminders of the power of community action.

So it's only a chair, but what a chair!

The Adirondack is a front-and-center seat into the creative process.

It talks of how things are dreamed up, worked up, changed,

tried out, changed some more, and how things,

just simple things,

become part of a living memory of a people.

★ ACKNOWLEDGMENTS ★

I gratefully acknowledge the dozens of people who helped me get this book finished over seven years (2000–2007). My children, Kendra, Jessica, and Eliza, grew up and left the house during that time. My wife, Theresa, patiently stayed. Thank you.

Members of the Thomas Lee family: Bruce Ware, Tony Ware, and Sandra Lee, have been gracious in their time, memories, and photographs. Historians and librarians in Saranac Lake, New York; Westport, New York; and Oldsmar, Florida, have moved the story back and forward with their research. Thanks to Phillip Gallos, Nona Hoskins, Rachael Lawrence, Marcia Tucker, Ted Comstock, Holly LiBaire, and Oldsmar Mayor Jerry Beverland. Also the librarians Jerrold Pepper at the Adirondack Museum and Carol Sanders at the Strong Museum in Rochester, New York.

I have been enthusiastically supported by dozens of makers of Adirondack chairs. Their names are scattered throughout this book.

In the world of publishing, I appreciate the help from Kevin Quirk of A Writer's Eye, agent Scott Mendel of Mendel Media Group, LLC, as well as my editors, Marisa Bulzone and Kristen Latta of Stewart, Tabori & Chang, and book designer Anna Christian.

Antique dealers Bert Savage, Barbara Pollack, John Wicks, and Ralph Kylloe have been very helpful.

Much of this book is indebted to the research of scholars: Craig Gilborn, Steven Gelber, Allan Gowans, Carolyn Goldstein, Ellen Boris, Sigfried Giedeon, and Lewis Mumford.

I have greatly appreciated my visits to places rich in Adirondack chairs: the Adirondack Museum in Blue Mountain Lake, New York; Wave Hill in Riverdale, New York; Innisfree Garden in Millbrook, New York; and the people, porches, and lawns of Block Island, Rhode Island, where this book was first imagined in the 1990s.

Photographs and art are courtesy of the following people and collections: Keith Levit: pages 2-3; Jacqueline Shaw: 4; Daniel Mack: 6, 12-13, 16, 17, 21, 45, 53, 57, 66, 67, 68, 69, 83, 84, 85, 89, 91, 93, 118, 119, 124-25; Ximagination: 7; Michael Gatewood: 18; V. J. Matthew: 19, 75, 77; Robert C. Tussey III: 25; Joy Brown: 28; Scott Pehrson: 30; Pierdelune: 33; Elena Elisseeva: 34; Zina Glazebrook: 35; Kalman Samelson: 36; Rago Arts and Auction Center: 41; Elpis Ioannidis: 42; Andrew McDonough: 43; Vaide Seskauskiene: 44; Bruce Wheadon: 44; The Adirondack Museum, Blue Mountain Lake, NY: 46; Library of Congress, LC-USZC2-4010: 47; Elizabeth Glasgow: 49; Sandra Lee: 54, 55; Ralph Atwell, Sr., Courtesy of Rachael Lawrence: 58; Ron Cosser: 58, 61; The Adirondack Museum, Blue Mountain Lake, NY: 60; Cassina USA: 63; Allentown Art Museum, Gift of Deborah S. Haight, 1997 (1997.006): 64; Treadway Gallery: 65; Steve Bowers: 70; Christies Images Ltd.: 71; CoverStock: 73; Joy Brown: 74; Donald Levin: 79; La-Z-Boy: 86; Shutterstock: 87; Jim Quinlan: 88, 89; John Fawcett: 95; Tim Healey, © John D. Wagner: 97, 98, 101, 102; Andrew Jackson: 105, 106, 107; Tyler W. Donald: 108; BRM Design: 109; Kam Ghaffari: 110; Roy Engelbrecht, Designs by Phillip Lazard, Jennifer Spendley, Vincent Thearle, Kevin Zimmerman, Nicole McHugh, and Chase DeForest: 112, 113, 119; Julie Morringello: 115; Paul Jacobsen: 116; Joseph Reboli: 116; Heidi Palmer: 116; Robert Cumming: 117; David H. Ramsey, Design by Nathan Rose: 119; Bobby Hansson, Design by Courtney Bowles: 119; Bruce Gray at brucegray.com: 120; Mark Mennin: 121; Barry Holden: 121; Joel Sisson: 122, 123; Robert Manley: 127.

"So You Want to Build an Adirondack Chair?" Text and illustrations adapted or based on material from *Building Adirondack Furniture* by John D. Wagner. Copyright © 1995 John D. Wagner. Used by permission of Williamson Books, an imprint of Ideals Publications.

★

Published in 2008 by Stewart, Tabori & Chang, an imprint of Harry N. Abrams, Inc.

Text copyright © 2008 by Daniel Mack

Library of Congress Cataloging-in-Publication Data:
Mack, Daniel.   The Adirondack: a celebration of a summer classic / Daniel Mack.   p. cm.
ISBN-13: 978-1-58479-568-1   ISBN-10: 1-58479-568-9
1. Lawn chairs. I. Title.   TS886.5.C45M33 2007   684.1'8—dc22

Editors: Marisa Bulzone and Kristen Latta   Designer: Anna Christian   Production Manager: Tina Cameron

The text of this book was composed in Adobe Garamond.

Printed and bound in China
10 9 8 7 6 5 4 3 2 1

HNA
harry n. abrams, inc.
a subsidiary of La Martinière Groupe
115 West 18th Street
New York, NY 10011
www.hnabooks.com